The Voice
In The Stillness

The Voice
In The Stillness

Messages and Lessons From The Creator

Jennifer L. Farley

BALBOA.
PRESS
A DIVISION OF HAY HOUSE

Balboa Press books may be ordered through booksellers or by contacting:

Balboa Press
A Division of Hay House
1663 Liberty Drive
Bloomington, IN 47403
www.balboapress.com
1-(877) 407-4847

Because of the dynamic nature of the Internet, any web addresses or
links contained in this book may have changed since publication and
may no longer be valid. The views expressed in this work are solely those
of the author and do not necessarily reflect the views of the publisher,
and the publisher hereby disclaims any responsibility for them.

The author of this book does not dispense medical advice or prescribe the use
of any technique as a form of treatment for physical, emotional, or medical
problems without the advice of a physician, either directly or indirectly. The
intent of the author is only to offer information of a general nature to help you
in your quest for emotional and spiritual well-being. In the event you use any
of the information in this book for yourself, which is your constitutional right,
the author and the publisher assume no responsibility for your actions.

Certain stock imagery © Thinkstock.
Any people depicted in stock imagery provided by Thinkstock are models,
and such images are being used for illustrative purposes only.

ISBN: 978-1-4525-4584-4 (e)
ISBN: 978-1-4525-4583-7 (sc)

Library of Congress Control Number: 2012901437

Printed in the United States of America

Balboa Press rev. date: 2/17/2012

Preface

I was raised amid the dark green forests and powerful ley lines of Washington State. From a very early age, I felt a deep connection to the Earth and The Creator. Playing under the giant canopies of pine, I always felt at home and in touch with God.

Constantly searching for my true purpose, I studied many religions, incorporating the best of each into my daily life. While continuing to work in the public sector, I discovered the book "Mutant Message Down Under" by Marlo Morgan. This was my first introduction to a world where things were known to be, given thanks for in advance and received with open, loving hearts.

I experienced my first ThetaHealing™ session in December 2007 and, in February of 2008, received a birthday gift that would change my life ~ Vianna Stibal's "ThetaHealing™—Go Up And See God/Go Up And Work With God". I devoured the book and, within the first two days, began making belief changes on myself.

For the first six months, I was self-taught. In June of 2008 I completed DNA 1 & 2, my Advanced ThetaHealing™ class in September 2008 and my DNA 1 & 2 teacher's certification in June 2011 to become a certified ThetaHealing™ Instructor. My two children have joined me in this wonderful journey and are certified as well.

In April of 2009, I began receiving messages from The Creator. At first they were sporadic, gradually picking up speed as I grew more attuned to listening for Creator's lessons and teaching tools. I began posting them and, much to my surprise, the reception they received was astounding! A friend suggested I put them into a book so, here it is.

Instructions for Use

This compilation can be used several different ways;

* A meditation tool. Choose a writing from the book and ask The Creator to show you what it means. Over the course of your day, keep an eye out for signs; they will appear!

* A once-a-day devotional. There is a Creator Writing for each day of the year.

* If you have a question, concern or challenging situation; focus on it, close your eyes and scroll through until you feel you need to stop. Your answer will be there.

The Creator has set up a learning in each writing. After you read it, say yes out loud, and the answer will be given to you in a way that you will most understand.

For

Michelle McLaughlan Muir ~ for being the first to suggest this wonderful project. Thank you my friend, you are always in my heart.

My children, Samuel Richard and Rachel Frances ~ for tolerating Mum's 'moments' and loving me even when I felt unlovable. You are the shining jewels in my life.

George and Jason French ~ there are bonds of blood and bonds of friendship. You were blessed with both. Thank you for showing me that you need not be in each other's company to love because time and space never changes it.

And finally ~ my Margarito ~ for teaching me what it means to truly trust. I love you always.

Your "growing time" may be perceived by your conscious mind as painful, irritating and frustrating. It is a necessary part of being human. You are expanding your awareness of what you are going to be to yourself, each other, and the world around you. The end result will always be satisfying.

If you choose to be someone's rock, be
sure they do not use you as a step to get
to something they perceive as better.

Trust. Trust yourself, trust the deep connection, trust that you are building something worthwhile, trust the faith I and others have placed in you, trust my love for you.

Breathe........breathe into yourself. Know that you are loved, cherished, honored, respected and admired. You are perfect and whole in my eyes, a shining light, a gift, a wonderful presence on your Earth-plane. Breathe, breathe into yourself and *know*.

Your most profound moments will be when you release 'what I was' and move into *'What I Am'*.

Reach beyond what you think is attainable!
Life has a way of exceeding your
expectations with one positive thought!

Only *you* can give *you* a sense of completeness.
Look within yourself and ask, "What am I lacking",
then ask me for it. Your wish is my command.

The light that shines within you will never be extinguished for you are a child of Creator and Co-Creator of your existence. You have been given, and *are,* a gift of unconditional love, joy, and truth, embracing each new day as a new beginning in your power, and being honored for the strong person you are.

When you reach what you believe to be your
highest pinnacle ~ you may look down at the
climb and congratulate yourself on the progress
you have made. But, if you look to the heavens
and say, "look how much further I can go",
that is when you make REAL progress.

Reach beyond what you thought possible.
Open yourself up to experience *this*
life, at *this* time, in *this* moment.

You have something to teach. You have something to learn. Many of you believe that they are two different things. They are wrapped together in a spiritual dance of intertwining energies. Everything you learn, you will eventually teach; and every time you teach, you learn something new.

A *true* teacher doesn't allow a student to become dependent on the teacher in any way.

Keep this in mind; you have been given the gift of free will, the ability to create whatever you choose. Everything you do, the words you utter, the thoughts you have, the smiles you give and all you look upon are moments of Creation. What do you want to create with your moments on your Earth-plane?

Rather than saying, "what does this person mirror in me", start with the *feeling* the actions triggered and explore from there. *"Jump over the mirror and into yourself"*. You'll be surprised at what you find!

It is time...........the calling together of your family.
It may not be the one you were born into, it may
not be the one you think. It is the family you are
being introduced to now, the family that will be
present at the "awakening time". Revel in the love
and support of that family, it is a joyous occasion!

To love and be loved, to experience and help others experience joy, to be true to yourself and recognize that truth in others ~ this is the master plan. This is my gift to you!

Say *yes* as often as possible..........to love, joy, truth, fun, and most of all, life! Your time on your Earth-plane is too short to let a no, a negative thought or action influence you!

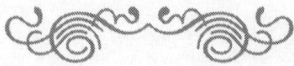

While you are here, remember to revel in your humanness! Very few of you choose to come to your Earth-plane. It can be challenging and painful but, it is also an experience of love, joy and truth. Learn well and have fun doing it!

Clarity comes from feeling, seeing and listening to the world around you. It is as natural as taking a breath.

To be seen and heard; see yourself as whole and complete and the world will see you that way. Speak your truth from the heart with strength and meaning - the world will listen.

Beauty, peace, patience, tranquility and love ~ this is what you are to me.

The way through the resistance in your heart is to become what it is resisting. Only when you can truly embrace the emptiest part and make it your own, can you say "I love unconditionally".

How you choose to experience the world depends
on how much you are willing to release. You can
hold onto your 'old experiences', letting them shape
and mold your *now,* or you can open yourself
up to the NOW and enjoy the experiences.

Reach down into the quiet place that exists
within. What do you hear? Listen to your
heart's song, it will tell you exactly what it
needs. Close your eyes. What do you see? Your
dreams will tell you what you will receive.

Every day, you are presented with things that remind you of your own Divinity and the Divinity of the Universe. Each one is a moment that will move your soul and become a part of the wonderful fabric that is you on your Earth-plane. Take a deep breath and say, "I expect it", and you will see!

To surrender; the ultimate act of ceasing to fight, to yield and allow yourself to participate in the flow of life. Let it become your liberating art, the sensual dance of unconditional love and trust in the Universe.

To change how you are perceived by yourself and others; be willing to pull yourself up and out of your old energy. Embrace the new and different with as much love as you embraced the old. It may be challenging and it may be painful, but it is the only way for change that has true meaning to occur.

Go to your center, your core and your soul in joy ~
for that is where I exist. Radiate that joy to the world
around you. You are the only one that knows how
to do it the way *you* do! If you all radiate joy in your
own way, there will be no dark corner left unlit.

Immerse yourself in the power of love! Love of self, love of each other, love of your world, love of *everything* you experience! Embrace the joy of *being* in love!

After the 'storm of introspection', there will
always be a peace that settles over your entire
being. Breathe it in and love yourself for the space
you are in now. Enjoy the quietness of your soul
because you've worked for and earned it.

Your thoughts are the palette from which you draw colors to paint your existence on your Earth-plane. Soft, bold, dark, light, broad strokes or fine lines, they are a part of your experience. Embrace and love them all....they are who you were, who you are and who you will become.

You have been given a powerful gift; the ability to build worlds, spin galaxies out of nothing, create civilizations and move mountains with a single thought. You can bring anything you want into existence. How you choose to use this gift is up to you.

Sometimes, the only 'trick' you need to
learn is to breathe. Just keep breathing.
The rest will fall into place.

Lay your hand upon your own chest and
know that you are touching love.

Experience each thought, take each breath, live each moment, love fully and with passion. Your existence on this Earth plane without passion is no existence at all.

The definition of *trust*; standing on the edge of
your own personal precipice, arms outstretched,
head back, wind kissing your face and *knowing*,
that when you leap, you already have the
knowledge of what it feels like to fly.

Express your deepest desires, your most heartfelt wishes, your dreams and your love. They cannot be fulfilled unless you give them 'action'.

Putting a wall around your deepest fears does nothing but hide them from yourself. Pull them out, turn them over in your hands, examine every detail, admire them for what they are and then release them with love. When the walls come down, the only thing left in its place will be joy.

Ask yourself at least once a day, "What do I want to be when I grow up"? The answer will change as you change.

How often to do you let *one fear* stand in your way of experiencing miracles? All of the joy, love, peace, abundance and exhilaration of your existence on your Earth plane await your forward motion.

Living in fear is perhaps your biggest asset, showing you exactly where you are. When you let go of it, you become what you truly *want* to be.

For just a few moments today, move away from your adult and revisit your child. Listen to how the wind blows, smell the sweetness of flowers, let your hands enjoy the different textures around you, look at your world through a child's eyes. Reacquaint yourself with beauty of curiosity and arousal. It is who you were born to be and who you really are.

Everything, absolutely everything that happens in
your life is for a reason. The joys and disappointments,
the love and let-downs, the happiness and fear.
There is a lesson in each. Take them for what they
are worth; an opportunity for you to grow.

How do you affect change in your life? Start from the beginning.

The *only* hero you can depend on is yourself!
If you cannot depend on yourself for your own
growth, there is no point in growing. Constantly
searching for an outside source does nothing
but enslave you to an unreachable ideal.

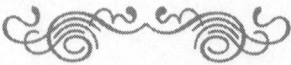

Just a reminder, lest you forget; you are human and have human emotions. That is why you chose to come to your Earth plane.....to have the experience of being *human*. If you deny your emotions, you deny your true purpose.

What do you wish to experience today? That
is up to you..........you make your Now.

Some of the easiest things to do are often perceived as the most challenging. Release yourself to the flow of the world around you, experience what you can; it is all a growth experience. You will be able to look back on it fondly and say, "I remember when.........".

Every day you are presented with opportunities that require choice. Do, don't do.....yes, no......experience, do not experience. Ask yourself, "is this in my highest and best"? Make a decision based on what your heart tells you. Then speak your truth. This is paramount. Whatever reaction you receive is secondary. Embrace the knowing that you have done what is best for you.

When things seem confusing or confounding,
take a step back and look at the infinite picture.
Things are not always what they appear to be
on the surface. Reality is a slippery concept.

What of emotional pain, physical pain and the like? As beings of light on your Earth plane, it is showing you a way to change how you see your existence. As always - you are given choices on what, where and how to see your world. Experience each moment with love and the full knowledge that, with each challenge, you are growing.

If you've ever said, "I have it/things under control", the
only person you are fooling is yourself. Relinquishing
control and going with the flow of things is the way
to find peace and a true understanding of yourself.

See and you will know. Love and you
will be free. Think and it is yours.

Look forward with anticipation to the coming
of each new day. Exciting experiences unfold,
wishes are granted and thoughts become reality,
all in the blink of an eye. Are you anticipating?

Doubts, disbeliefs, fears, insecurities, sadness,
pain and lack are all pointers. Experiencing them
shows you exactly what you need to change. You
are given a choice; wrap them around yourself
like a blanket, content to live with them forever,
or release them with love. Free will is yours.

What *was* is past. What *is* may not be what your perception of it is. What *is to be*..........now that is where you get to have some fun and Create!

Take a moment and enjoy the peaceful quiet of your soul. When the jangling from the outside world ceases, you will be able to connect to the within and without. Relax into the joy of it all and let it carry you through your day.

Listen to your heart and soul. They are your Divine guides, your most enthusiastic partners in this wonderful dance of life!

Even when you feel you are not; know that you are protected, admired, nurtured and loved.

Infinity and all of its gifts of love, joy, beauty, happiness, abundance, truth and any other thing you can think of are available to you. The only thing holding it back is your ability to imagine it as yours.

Even with all of what you perceive as your imperfections, you are perfect. You are doing exactly what you should be doing at this very moment in time. Know that you are loved, honored, protected, cherished, respected and thought of very highly by the people you have chosen to surround yourself with at this time in your life. Be proud of who you are. I am.

These are the three things to remember when challenging situations present themselves in your life; reaching, stretching, growing.

If you listen carefully enough, you'll hear the Universe singing its 'Ode to Joy' to you. It's the turning of your Earth, the starry skies, the wind blowing, the clouds and the very air that you breathe. Let your body be filled with its song.

Listen to the sound of your own
heartbeat......it is my voice.

Move away from 'linear thinking'. There is so
much more to your existence than getting from
Point A to Point B. Instead, think of yourself as
a red dot on a map; YOU.......ARE.........HERE.

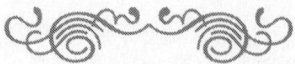

The time has come to move beyond what you are into what you will become. The transition will be well worth the effort.

When you believe that things are starting to spin too fast...take a deep breath, focus on the truth and smile. You are the way you are because you are intended to be that way.

Remember to look for the unexpected gifts. Experienced personally or witnessed from afar, they are all around you. A smile, a comfortable pause in a conversation, the way a child laughs or a loving glance between two people. They are to remind you that your existence on your Earth plane is full of miracles.

Love comes in all shapes, sizes and packages.
There are no boundaries, no limits on what
you can experience if you are open to it.

You are Master of your Existence, your World and your Universe..........dream, build and create with love!

How beautiful are you; as beautiful as the sky full of stars. How loved are you; as infinitely as anyone can be loved. How cherished are you? You are my perfect gift to your Earth plane because in you exists everything that I am.

You've chosen to come to this Earth plane for a specific
purpose; to be one that has never existed before,
does not exist anywhere else now and will never exist
again. You are unique, special and a joy to behold!

Like the sea, you will experience an ebb and flow
to your life. The sea knows its own rhythmic
nature and wants for nothing else than to continue
its journey. So should you remember yours.

When you have your 'moments', remember; the sun still shines above the clouds, the rivers still flow to the sea and the path you are on now is the right one.

Allow yourself to see what others see in you.

The most important relationship you will ever have is with yourself. If you are ready, willing and able to love every part of you, you are truly ready to love another.

There is no limit to what the human heart can take or the amount of love it can experience.

You are always given a choice; create separateness where none exists or embrace the fact that, as part of a whole, you are always connected to one another. Being separate only serves the person creating it, an insulation that is temporary at best. Strengthen your connection to the Earth, your fellow man and to the people that care for you. Therein lays your true freedom.

Oh, if you could see and experience the beauty I see in you! Ever expanding into your light, shining brighter with every second, every moment and every breath you take. You are truly perfect! Open yourself up to it!

Those around you may not understand your 'gifts'.........yet. The time will come when you are called upon to be assistants in the Great Divine Awakening. Use this time to show as much love, compassion and understanding as you possibly can. The practice is a stepping stone in your growth.

Light workers; Children of God, Spirit, Infinite
Oneness and any other name you choose to use; work
together, embrace and take care of each other with
love, understanding and compassion. You will all
be needed because the time of the "early awakened"
is at hand and it will be a joyous occasion!

Closely examine your 'inner workings' to decide what you do and do not need to keep. All the things you *thought* you needed for protection, comfort or love will not be important anymore. In your ever expanding awareness, there will always be something more beautiful to come and take its place. The 'old ones' had it right when they said, "Ask and you shall receive".

Things can change in an instant. What was important will suddenly have no impact on your Earth-plane existence. Once again, you have the choice; mourn the loss of the old or embrace the new. The decision is yours.

You are all part of the great cycle - birth, life, death and rebirth. The lessons from each experience are of great value in depth, breadth and scope. Learn, learn, learn and grow!

You cannot force the 'dreamers' to open their eyes.
All you can ask is that they do it in their own time
and in a way that is in their highest and best.

Even for those of you on the 'enlightened path', there will be times where you do not feel particularly enlightened or uplifted. This is not something that needs to be 'fixed', 'controlled' or 'managed'.......it is to be experienced! You are, after all, an Earth-plane inhabitant feeling Earth-plane feelings. Treat it as the shore treats the ocean's waves.....they come and they go. Simple.

Some of your most profound growth will not come from your happy 'moments' but, from your disappointments. Moving past them and into *more* of what you are becoming is part of your experience. Embrace and love each one..........they love you.

Too often you let the war within take over the flow
of the Universe. Head/heart, logical/illogical, right/
wrong, good/evil, close/distant, love/hate........
none of this really matters. When the war is over,
the Universe is still waiting, as calm and quiet
as it has ever been, for your return to peace.

How you move forward depends on how 'static'
you choose to remain in certain areas of your
life. If all but one part is freed, it is for naught.
Release the frozen part of you, tear down the walls
and knock down the battlements. Even in your
vulnerability, you will always be protected.

Open your heart to all possibilities! You are a
perfect child of the Universe.....nothing is beyond
your grasp, comprehension or abilities.

When you are wrapped up in a moment of your reality, things can seem very far away, unattainable and out of reach. Breathe into the moment and let it pass. Earth-existence is a very transitory space and will change in an instant if you only let it.

It is important to remember that everyone 'awakens' at their own pace. Don't rush yourself or others, there is plenty of time.

The Universe will speak to you in a myriad of different ways. It can be something moves your soul, touches your heart, amazes you, or truly makes you think. They are all around you. When you learn to recognize them, you will see!

Suspend your disbelief and all things become possible!

One thing will set you apart from all others; the ability to stop, quiet your mind, heart and body, to revel in your connection to the Universe. Be the calm in the storm of people running away, to or from.

Lest you forget; you are the Divine..............animated.

You are moving forward faster than you ever thought possible. Now is the time to decide what you want to keep and what you want to let go. What does not serve you will only hold you back from your intended purpose. Let go of your darkness and stand in your light - that is where you are most beautiful!

It is time to step into who you are going to be and into your *I Am*. See yourself as I see you; perfect, whole, beautiful and shining brightly!

Some of you may find yourself caught up in the grief of what is passing. In the infinite picture, this is a minimal change. Rejoice in the lessons you have learned and the things you have taught others. Without them, you would not be who you are today and what you will become tomorrow.

During this wonderful time of change, it is important to remember what you need. Settling for anything less than what you truly need, want and deserve is diminishing. Step up, embrace who you will become and love yourself. After all, it has to start somewhere, why not with you?

Remember, when power struggles rage around you
like a hurricane, you are the eye of the storm, the
calm quiet. You are so much stronger than you think.
Embrace your peacefulness. In your connection
with the Universe, no harm will come to you.

You deserve the best your Earth-plane has to offer. Embrace it. Settling for anything less is a disservice to your *'I Am'*.

Stand in, embrace and love your truth. It may
be one of the most challenging things you
ever do; however, it is most rewarding.

When others react with sadness/disbelief/ anger when you speak your truth, remember that it is not your sadness/disbelief/anger. If you have spoken your truth with pure love and intent, the rest will take care of itself.

Live in truth, love in truth and be at peace with truth. You are Divine Truth in human form.

The higher vibration and shining of your light is your soul singing to the Universe. Follow your own tempo, your own beat. There is nothing else like it. It is pure magic!

A power struggle is a war with yourself. Control is
attempting to 'move' a situation to a place where
you want it to be. Neither serves any purpose.
Let go of the power struggles and the control;
a most wondrous thing will happen; you will
be at peace and centered within yourself.

For those of you that spend your time looking for outward signs of magic and miracles; there is no need. It already exists in you!

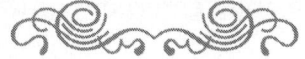

You are not meant to have a singular existence.
Together as one, as a whole, is how great things
are accomplished on your Earth-plane.

Embrace the truth of others in the same way you embrace your own. Love them for trusting you, love yourself for listening. It need not become a part of your existence unless you really want it to be. It is just another facet to the gem of free will.

The beauty in your life comes not from the connections you make but, the relationships you have.

Step out of the endless loop of what you are
and onto the path of what you will become.
Uncharted territory, though not familiar, carries
with it a myriad of rewards never imagined!

You will inherently gravitate and draw to
you whatever your thought patterns create.
Negative draws negative, positive draws positive.
Which would you like to possess today?

The Lion's Gate has opened. It is imperative to stand in your honesty and integrity at this time. Know that your truth to yourself and others is of the utmost importance. If you choose to stand in integrity, it will show in your life immediately.

Expecting others to change to fit your needs, wants and desires is futile. The only thing you can truly change is what is within *you*.

You are ever-expanding beings of The Universe. When you choose to finish experiencing 'negative', the only thing you will be able to draw is 'positive'. Allow yourself time for this growth and know that you are being watched over with loving eyes.

Do you realize *why* you chose to come to your Earth-plane? You came to have *fun*! Being 'enlightened' does not always have to be mundane, even or quiet. Laugh; take joy in the bodies you inhabit, smile, *play*!

Surrender.... To some it means to give up, to give control to another, to subjugate yourself; the exact opposite is true. To surrender is to give yourself over to the flow of The Universe knowing that whatever happens, all will be well and in your highest and best.

Reasoning your faults and shortcomings does not make them go away; it just puts them on hold.

Your reactions to any given situation depend on what growth stage you are in. The more you step into your light; there will be a lessening of the need to react to other's behaviors. You are moving closer to your center.

Be present in every hour, minute, second and
in every breath you take in your Earth-plane
existence. All the lessons, experiences, love
and friendship you could ever want is there in
those moments. Do not let them pass you by.

Strive to find your connectedness to The
Universe within and without yourself. Once
in place, connectedness to other Earth-
plane beings becomes second-nature.

From the beginning, from the moment you drew your first breath on your Earth-plane, you were whole. Life experiences changed and morphed you from that wholeness. You now have an opportunity to return to it. Grab it with both hands and pull it close to you. It is, after all, yours.

There is a time and a place for everything. The place for joy, laughter, love, fun and play is *now*!

Yes, the possibilities for your Earth-plane existence are endless. You are only limited by your imagination. Dream, dream big and dream it into your reality.

If you ask yourself if you are really hearing
the voice of The Universe, then you are not.
Whenever The Universe speaks, it speaks
volumes of truth and there is no denying it.

Shifts in your perception are inevitable. They are your signs; 'growth in progress'. What you choose to do with them is completely up to you.

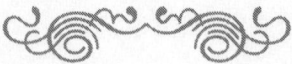

In being responsible for yourself, you will innately
be aware of your responsibility to others.

When you move from a place of wanting to 'push' things to a state of wanting to 'be', the quiet will be all-enveloping. This is not something to fear. Enjoy the ability to be completely and utterly immersed in The Universe, it is where true peace exists.

If you allow yourself to be bent or allow others to bend you to their will through spoken or unspoken expectation, it is a recipe for disaster and self-loathing. Stay true to who you are and what you want from your Earth-plane existence. Stand in integrity, it is the true path to what you want to accomplish.

You often forget how to look past the superficial and less important. The Universe will always tell you what to let go of and what to go forward with. Connections are connections; they serve a purpose in everyday life but never give you what you truly need. The fulfillment of your soul comes from relationships with those you love, appreciate and respect - they last lifetimes.

Life is not stagnant but fluid.....it changes, it
evolves, it grows. You can remain in your own
paradigm, continuing to exist in the world you
created for yourself 'before' *or* you can be fluid;
change, evolve and grow. Release your fear of
being fluid and so shall your life become.

The fear of the unknown is not a fear at all. The fear exists in how you feel you will act in and react to it. People constantly change and so will the situations. Why hold onto the fear of an ever-changing reality? Let go............just be..............and all will be well.

By refusing to step into whatever you may consider 'something serious', you are sending a very clear message to yourself and others; I am not worth being taken seriously. If this is how you choose to be perceived, wonderful, but who wants to be a 'clown' forever?

If you have to ask, "what do I do now?", "where should I be going?", "how do I handle this?" or "what do you want from me?" you are not listening to The Universe - you are trying to rely only on yourself. You receive signs, pointers, read or hear something every day that shows you. Quiet yourself, truly listen with your heart, it is all there......*listen*!

If you find yourself mired and lost in the maze of your 'old energy', your 'old life', your 'old ways'....... that is a sign that it is time for a change. Why do you hesitate? Step forward, embrace it, it is yours.

If I were to stand right in front of you and say,
"This is what you should do", would you listen? It
is no different than when I speak to you through
The Universe. I say to you now, "this is what you
should do..........open your heart to The Universe
and *listen*! You will always receive the truth".

Forcing an issue, trying too hard to change the outcome or ignoring The Universe is the 'old way' of doing things. Slow down, take a deep breath and........ flow! There is no need to be stuck where you are. The entire Universe is at your disposal, take advantage of it.

In angry retort, humans will often say, "who do you think you are"? Well, I am you.....you are me.........we are one. To deny that fact and continue to view yourself as singular is the most common mistake you will make on your Earth-plane. Learn from your mistakes, know that everyone is your mirror and derive great joy from the thought that you have learned something new today.

You will truly know joy when you have the *freedom* of joy! You will truly know *love* when you have the *freedom* of love! You will truly know yourself when you have the *freedom* of self!

So much on your Earth-plane is changing so quickly that you may feel it is difficult to keep up. What was once comfortable, familiar and made you feel safe no longer exists. Why continue in your 'old ways'? They will, very soon, be obsolete. This is the time of the new reality, this is your time, and this is *the* time of change.

Everything you need is within you.

When you are ready to accept the best, The Universe will provide you with the best.

When others hurt, demean, bruise your self-esteem or present any other undesirable human trait remember; you are not being attacked. They are attacking themselves.

What you expect may not be exactly what you get. Keep
your heart, mind and thoughts open to the experience
that things change and change quickly. Every person
on your Earth-plane has that capability and will
often surprise you when you give them a chance.

Like a moat around a castle; you protect yourself.
To tear down the unnecessary walls, you must
resist digging the moat deeper. It is a distraction
to keep you from getting to the *real* point.

What you are expecting might not be exactly what you get. Sometimes, your highest and best requires you receiving much, much more!

The ones truly meant to stand beside you are often waiting in the wings, watching silently. They've been there all along; smiling at your successes, cheering when you accomplish your goals, loving you when you feel unlovable and sending healing when you feel you have crashed. Turn around, look behind you and you'll see them gazing at you with all the love in the world.

Where does all this 'need' come from? The Universe has already gifted you, yet most spend their time looking *around* it to see what is beyond. Is there something 'beyond'? Yes, probably. However, constantly looking for outside sources of happiness, love and human fulfillment keeps you separate and isolated. Look within to what you already have, you are complete. Embrace it.

The three most useful things you will ever do;
watching, waiting and listening. All will be revealed.

When you free yourselves of negative emotions
like doubt, fear and anger, a strange and
lovely experience will occur... freedom.

When you finally release the need to 'feed' off of others in the form of garnering praise, receiving self-esteem boosts or being wanted by them then you will be ready for the *real* healing to begin.

Stand in your truth. All will be well.

If you did one thing every day that you said you could not do, what could you accomplish? How many problems would be overcome? How many mountains could be moved? How many obstacles scaled? All it takes is one thought, one step, one action.

You can spend all day weighing the pros and cons of any given situation. If you listen to your heart, my Voice incarnate, it will always give you the truth.

Wake up to your own possibilities as ever-expanding beings of Light. Everything is within your reach and within your realm of imagining.

Every challenging decision you have to make is a culmination of your life experiences. You can continue to let your past affect your decisions or forge a new future for yourself. Free will is always yours.

Love is the least understood human emotion on this Earth-plane. It is wrapped up in everything you do and say. And, unfortunately, most view it as a binding, chain or hook. However, if you let love flow in the way The Universe intended, anything is possible.

It is all laid out before you; the beauty, the love, the joy and the excitement of living on your Earth-plane. Why dwell in the pain of the past when all the goodness in the world awaits you?

How can you say you love another if you do not love yourself? How can you say you love yourself if you do not love another? It is a paradox to be sure. In the ebb and flow of your Earth-plane existence, in the flow of Love through The Universe, they become one and the same.

The gentle hand of The Universe will always
guide you in the right direction.

It is so easy...............it really is. You make it 'hard' because you *think* it has to be that way. Breathe, just breathe. The rest will follow!

Sometimes, you just have to get out of your own way.

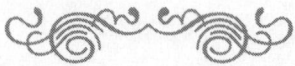

Forced happiness does not make happiness.
Forced joy does not make joy. When you can feel
these emotions without question and without ego
then they are real in your Earth-existence.

Self-examination is one of the most challenging things you can do on your Earth-plane. By loving your 'thorns', you can choose to continue to present them or eliminate them.

Live each moment of your Earth-plane existence with intent and purpose. So much joy and knowledge can be gained, so much love spread............why wait?

The one thing I have noticed; you spend a lot of time reaching, reaching, and reaching to touch 'beyond'. Everything you need already exists within you! Reach *in* and touch Divinity.

Oftentimes, you will ask yourself, "Why am I being treated this way"? The answer is very simple......
you allow it. If you treat yourself with love, kindness, respect, passion and joy, others will follow suit.

You came here to experience being human. Being human is all about growth. To deny that growth is to deny the ultimate purpose of being human.

You're on a ledge overlooking a beautiful mountain lake. It is a gorgeous day and so hot! But, you are standing there quaking in fear of the breathtakingly cold water. What are you going to do, wait there until the beauty of the day fades? Or jump in knowing, that once you're in the water, it will feel wonderful.

For every time you cried out to the sky for
help, I was there. For every joyous moment you
experienced, I was there. Why? Because they
are one in the same to me. Every human moment
you have on your Earth-plane is Divine.

Every experience you are presented with is
an opportunity to stretch beyond what you
currently are and into what you will become.

It is very easy to be one of many. It's a gift to be one in a million. You *are* one in a million to me.

What an amazing being you are! You are hurt and you recover, you sing and others smile, you smile and The Universe is a better place because of you!

Step back and take a look at yourself. Are you where you want to be, doing what you want to do, living the life you want to live, loving who you want to love and being loved for who you are? You can, you know. All it takes is *one step*.

Letting go of what you thought, moving into what *is* and further into what you can become is very powerful. Claim your power as Divine Beings on your Earth-plane!

Every set back you experience is a jumping off point to start a new reality for yourself. Take a big deep breath, a high bounce on the board and *go*!

In the beginning, there was *love*.

If you begin with love, from a place of love,
the only thing that will grow is *love*!

You may reach a point when you have to choose between love of self and love of another in spite of yourself. One reclaims your power, the other gives it away. What you choose is ultimately up to you and how you want to live the remainder of your existence on your Earth-plane; empowered or enslaved.

Of all the decisions you make on a daily basis, how many are based on passion? Next to love, this emotion carries with it the strongest manifestation possibilities available in your Earth-plane existence. Do everything you do with passion; it exists in pure truth.

How? What? When? Where? Why? These
are all inconsequential questions. Know
that you have it and it is yours.

In saying what you need to say with honesty,
integrity, love, passion, sincerity and feeling;
you will have spoken your truth.

You are *human*. You came for the *human* experience.
Some of the things you are faced with are challenging
but must run their course. It is *your* choice to hold
onto them (be enslaved by them) or release them
with love (become empowered from them) and grow.
You will never forget those experiences however;
you will become a better person for them.

How to transcend the physical world while
existing in a physical body; *Believe*!

Pain is holding onto something that no longer serves you. Thank it for teaching you it's valuable lessons and release it to The Universe to be transmuted back to love. You will then be free to reach 'beyond'.

You do not realize it most of the time but, by just being you, you bring magic into everyday life.

Standing in your truth is the purest form of self-love.

How often do you tell yourself, "I am exceptional, I am beloved, and I am beautiful"? You should do this every day because, every day, this is what you are to me.

Being solitary does not mean isolation. It is a 'getting to know yourself' time, a time to embrace and find out what you really mean to yourself. It is not loneliness; it is reacquainting yourself with an old friend.

There is magic all around you. Do not let the joy of what you consider 'little things' escape your notice.

Now is the time! Stand up, be strong in your beliefs and show the world what you are made of. Throw your arms in the air and shout, *"I am alive"*!

All of the doubt, fear, hatred, loathing, pain and hurt
you carry can be erased by the joyful knowing that,
through it all, you are loved, honored, cherished,
respected and admired for exactly who you are.

Stop! Stop running and spinning in circles, just stop. Let the vertigo subside and look at your surroundings. What do you see? The path you need to be on is right there, right in front of you! Put one foot in front of the other in forward motion and your goals *can* be accomplished.

To say, "I love you" to another without
expectation is the greatest gift you can give
yourself. When you come from a place of love
to give love, you will receive love in return.

When you detach emotionally, you are really detaching from yourself. You chose your Earth-plane existence to experience human emotions. By 'removing' yourself, you are denying the very reason you are here. By embracing all, you grow.

Release your attachments to what was and what will be. They only serve to confuse and confound you. Instead, relish each moment you can draw a breath!

It is all a matter of perspective; you can
view your Earth-plane existence as work
or you can view it as play. You are, after all,
here for the experience are you not?

For those of you that still feel like you are 'living through hell on Earth'; do not despair. The Universe always provides you with what you need. Just ask and each moment from this one forward will be filled with more joy than you will ever be able to describe.

If you are constantly looking 'outside' for fulfillment, there will always be 'something more' you need. If you look within, to what The Universe placed there in the beginning, that is where you will find your true happiness.

As you grow spiritually, some of you may view your bodies as something to despise; heavy, cumbersome packages that no longer serve you. In embracing your Earth-plane existence in its entirety (including your body), there will be no need to 'escape' into your mind. Everything you need is right there.

Sometimes, the hardest 'mountains'
to climb are the smallest.

If you always wait for the right time to move forward, you will be waiting forever. Do not think.....*know*! Take that *first* step into joy, compassion, life and love!

Logic, deductive reasoning, intellect; this is your Earth-plane language. But, do not dismiss feeling, emotion and intuition. This is how The Universe speaks to you.

I am grateful for every moment you choose to stay
and continue your Earth-plane existence. The lessons
you learn, your experiences, the love you share
and the way you grow are a constant joy to me!

Can you look at yourself and say, "I love me! I love
my good and my not so good. I love my bright parts
and my thorns."? If I, as The Universe, can say
that then so should you be able. It is not 'difficult'
or 'hard', it just is. I love you just as you are.

When you were a child and asked your parent, "Am I growing?" and they said yes, you believed them. It is the same thing now. Just because you cannot see, hear, feel, touch or taste it does not mean it is not happening. If you ask me, "Am I growing?" I can tell you yes, you are. Your Earth-plane existence is not always about experiencing, sometimes it is just knowing.

You were created in love and with love by The Universe.
Why try to be anything other than what you are?

Mired in, wallowing in, stuck in..........what do
these mean? It is your conscious mind's way of
saying, "I refuse to move for you". Go into your
heart and ask there. The Universe will always
know and teach you a way of freeing yourself.

Long after you are gone, every part of you
will continue to resonate through everything
you have touched, looked at and experienced.
How will you choose to be remembered?

Naiveté and innocence are qualities to be admired, not admonished. When you can continue to view your Earth-plane existence through the eyes of a child, great things can be accomplished.

Embrace yourself without reservation, conditions or boundaries. Embrace others with love, knowing that you can give them what you give yourself.

If you approach your 'attachments' with the thought of finding your other half, neither of you will ever be complete. The Universe intended two wholes to make a whole. In knowing and loving yourself fully, you are then able to experience another in the same way.

There is nothing that compares to the sensual
ecstasy of your existence. It is pure magic.

You have been given a human body; the most efficient thing ever created. Along with it come emotions, reactions and other, sometimes very unexpected, things. Rather than spending time 'stifling' whatever comes, allow yourself to *experience* and be in the flow of The Universe.

Show your joy to the world and it will
reflect back to you ten-fold!

Do you exist in a paradox of pretenses, games, lies, wanna-be attitudes, insecurities or falsehoods? Strip all of this away and all you are left with is you. You can be safe in the knowledge that you are exactly how The Universe intended you to be. There is none better on the face of your planet.

Take time to explore all of the wonderful
nuances of your Earth-plane existence.

You talk of attaining bliss, striving for the goal of
*BE*ingness and fighting to find the quiet within like
it is your 'employment'. The Universe has never made
things that 'hard'. All you have to do is breathe, that
is it, that is all...........just breathe and magic happens.

The Universe gives you the tools, have fun
learning to use them. Like a child and their
beloved imagination; color, paint with fingers and
brushes, draw, sing, dance, jump, run.....*create* the
existence you want. Never mind what you appear
to be to others in the process or how much talent
you feel you have, just play for the joy of it all!

You will reach a place where you can say, "I love you" to someone (male or female) without conditions, expectations or a need for anything more than to honor them as human. It may be misinterpreted by those who are not able to grasp the concept of what you are really saying........yet. Do not be disheartened by their fear. Just continue to love; it is all that you are and what you were created to do.

Breathe............just breathe. That is the only thing you have to do right now. When you get up in the morning and take that first conscious breath, know that all the others will follow suit. Everything is going to be wonderful and perfect and right and OK. Just breathe.

In releasing your fear, you become more of what
The Universe intended you to be - whole.

Time; be willing to give yourself infinite
amounts of it to learn what you need to learn.

There is a lot to be said about getting out of your own way. Sometimes, you just have to step aside and let The Universe do all the work.

What do you want to be when you grow up? For a child, a simple question with infinite possibilities. As you've grown into your Earth-plane adulthood, how many of them passed you by? It is not too late. Ask yourself, "What do I want to be when I grow up" then create, create, create! The infinite possibilities are still there, use them.

Devote time to discovering and awakening the Divine God/Goddess within. The ways of 'the warrior' are coming to an end. It is time to embrace your Universal gifts.

The rain does not know why it falls, the flower does not know why it blooms and the bird does not know why it sings. They do these things simply because it is what they do. Become like the rain, the flower and the bird; do....simply because you are.

You see yourself as where you live, to whom you are 'attached', who your friends are, where you have been, what you have experienced in the past and what you are experiencing now. The Universe sees you as you really are; a beautiful being of light; whole, complete, perfect.

You walk your own path and others walk theirs. This is the way it has always been. Enjoy *your* path and the company of the people that join you. Release the rest with love and support them on their journey.

If you didn't long for it from the beginning, you would never have chosen to come to your Earth-plane. There are lessons to be learned, things to be experienced and joy to be had. You requested it, therefore you are here. Embrace it with everything in your being.

Love with reckless abandon, like your
life depends on it. Because it does!

Stepping out of your dark well of despair and into
the light may seem painful at first; too bright,
too much, too soon. But, once you are breathing
in the honey-tasting air and love is all around
you, you will wonder why you ever doubted
stepping out at all. And the first time you reach
your arms and out touch the sky.........*bliss*!

Who are you? You are my greatest
gift to your Earth-plane.

Be yourself. That has always been the only thing The Universe wants of you.

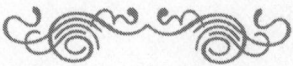

Love, Beauty, Truth.............strive to be these and you will have fulfilled your purpose on your Earth-plane.

As softly as a mother kisses her sleeping child,
as sweetly as a lover touches their beloved......
so should you be kind to yourself. If you do not
treat yourself well, how will you truly know
what it feels like when it comes to you?

Like a spider's web, you are all connected to one another through and with love..........sometimes, it takes the morning dew to see the whole 'picture'.

If you think you are a 'master of your existence', you have missed the whole point of being on the Earth. A true master knows they are continually the student.

Oh, if you only knew how easy it is to love for love's sake. My cherished one, it is the truest expression of appreciation, support, encouragement and respect that one human can give another.

Remember dear one; where love exists,
there is no fear.........there is *only Love*.

As always, you have a choice; you can mourn those
that chose to cross over or celebrate who they
were in their Earth-plane existence. Returning
to The Universe has always been a joyous
occasion regardless of the mode of crossing.

Truly enjoy the moments of peace, contentment, inner-quiet and joy you experience. They are the mile markers of your Earth-plane existence.

When you connect with another human being, there is a magic that happens, a dancing of your two souls. The dance makes your Earth-plane existence worthwhile.

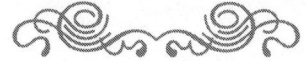

Make music with the movement of your human body,
make every smile you give like the stars shining,
make every moment of your Earth-plane existence
like magic. Show the world the beauty of your soul.
Be in rapture of the wonderful gift you call life.

Sensuality does not exist solely in the physical world. Embrace the sensuality of your soul. Release the fear of exploring the true nature of The Universe within.

When people are not truthful about you it means
they cannot be honest about or with themselves.
Take heart in knowing that you know the truth
about you. Nothing can take that away.

Nothing is hard.........nothing is difficult...........nothing is hurtful. Everything is easy. Be everything!

The separation you create by feeling you have
to handle everything on your own is just that,
separation. Know that you exist on this Earth-plane
to love and support yourselves as well as others.

It is perfectly O.K. to be scared, angry, frustrated, sad, lonely or isolated. These things only become issues when you decide, within your own free will, to continue to hold onto and feed them. Treat each of these emotions as if you are a rock in the middle of a stream; let the water flow around you, knowing it will only touch you momentarily before continuing its journey.

You can stick your fingers in your ears and say, "la la la la la la la" for only so long. Eventually, you will have to wake up and listen.

If you truly and faithfully express yourself, there is no question of who you are to yourself and others.

What you believe to be true at this moment is a resting point on your way to further growth. You are a constantly changing, evolving being of light; there is no end to the truth you can attain.

Let the 'little moments' of your Earth-plane existence stir your soul and bring you to a higher awareness of you.

Recurring patterns in your life are The Universe pointing out to you what you need to change. Exercise your free will. Hold onto them and remain in your particular paradigm or release them to be transmuted and grow. The choice is *always* yours.

Sometimes the most profoundly verbal
moments are the quietest.

There will be times when you have to release and
trust the awakening process. It may not be an easy
thing to do, especially when a connection exists.
Let others know you are there, offer support when
asked and hold space for them in a kind, loving
manner. The rest is up to them and The Universe.

Compassion is not measured in the depth
of emotion you feel, it is in the depth of
emotion you let *others* experience.

Never forget; you are an Angel to someone!

When you speak softly, it can be as a lion's roar.

Faith and *trust* seem to be the two most challenging words for you to understand. Faith is trusting what you cannot see, trust is having faith in what you can.

What you live and feel, you draw to you. If
you live in thoughts of fear, desperation, hate,
poverty or blame The Universe will oblige. If
you choose to live in peace, love, abundance,
responsibility, integrity and truth; The Universe,
again, will oblige. Exercise your free will!

You being you is enough. When you stop trying to fit into other people's molds, you become the You that The Universe intended.

For those of you in a constant struggle, remove the fight and the fight ceases to exist in your paradigm.

Societal programming has made you keenly aware
of this thought; taking care of and thinking about
yourself first makes you selfish. Only when you can
truly take care of and think of yourself first, can
you do it for others. It is the first step to self-love.

If you become passionately in love with
your Earth-plane existence, there will
be no room for anything else.

Make every waking moment, everything you do
and every breath you take an act of prayer, love,
gratitude and thankfulness to The Universe.
Therein will you find your true peace.

What is keeping you? The Universe is waiting with open loving arms for you and your light. Step into and be enfolded in the embrace of unconditional love.

It can be challenging to see and let others walk their own path. To you, it may seem hurtful, painful or destructive. To them, it is just another lesson they need to learn. Bless their journey and release your attachment with unconditional love.

How will you know when it is time to stay put, move forward, release self-imposed bonds or walk away from a situation that is not serving you? Take a moment, focus on the infinite peace of The Universe and listen. The answer will come into your heart. That is where my Voice resides.

Leave whatever little darkness is left in you
behind and step into the light of The Universe.

This has been said many different ways, but here is a gentle reminder; play like you are five years old, love as if love were going to disappear tomorrow, dream your wildest dreams, laugh, smile and embrace your Earth-plane existence. Joy is yours!

You will reach a point when who loves you or who does not love you is no longer important. At that time you can say, "I am love, therefore, it is enough".

In spite of your faults, hang-ups and attachments
as well as any pain, sorrow and sadness you
may experience I still see you; the wondrous,
exquisite, unalterable beauty of you.

Give love, send love, receive love, become love and The Universe responds in kind.

Take every single wonderful, inspiring, supportive,
loving, caring, kind and sensitive thing anyone
has ever said to you and stretch it to infinity;
that is what The Universe knows you to be!

Your worthiness is not determined by what others feel or say about you, but how you feel and what you say about yourself.

The most rewarding thing you can ever
be is to be something to yourself.

The funny thing about love is it is unconditional and there is an infinite amount of it, but most humans are afraid to truly immerse themselves in it. Why? Because most of what you have experienced to this point has been purely conditional in nature. If you let go and trust it, as you trust The Universe, you would see there is nothing to fear. Release the fear and you will grow in your expression of love.

It is not necessary to understand why others do what they do. Free yourself of the attachments to the outcome of their behavior. And, if it does not serve you, wrap them in unconditional love and send them to The Universe to be cared for in their highest and best.

What you think is easy initially, ends up being the most challenging thing you have experienced thus far. Your Earth-plane existence calls for a bit of bush-whacking on occasion. "Off the beaten path" is far more interesting.

Inertia means that an object will always continue moving at its current speed and in its current direction until some force causes its speed or direction to change. *Be your own inertia!*

Leave yourself open to the experience of falling in love with something, someone or some idea every day. One of your greatest joys on this Earth-plane is your infinite ability to enjoy and embrace the feeling of love.

Your transition from lower to higher vibrations is complex and yet so simple. It is predestined. You chose it before you arrived on your Earth-plane.

You do not have to 'know' all of what is transpiring on a conscious level. Be at peace and know that your soul is doing exactly what it should be doing at this particular moment in time.

The need to change another being into something
they are not, to suit your needs, is a need that exists
within *yourself*. Do not ask the other person to change.
They are perfect in and with their imperfections.
Instead, change what *you* feel *they* need to change.
We are mirrors for each other. Embrace it with love.

Radiant soul, being of light; from your lips, words of truth and love are uttered with profound quietness.

You will know when the time is right to stay still and quiet or move forward, to fight or surrender, to be static or grow. You will know. Just listen.

Emotional, mental or physical pain is
The Universe's way of telling you 'stop
doing that, it is not good for you'!

Be responsible for yourself and your
actions. In doing so, you set an example
for others. *That* is where it begins!

You have nothing to fear of love. Love is
all, love is nothing, love exists within you,
without you and throughout The Universe.
All you have to do is embrace it!

Emotions are not meant to be erased or 'controlled', they are meant to be experienced. It is part of your Earth-plane existence. Treat them as waves on the shore, they come and go, nothing more.

Be grateful for the waves of emotion as
they happen. They are who you are!

Joy, peace, love and acceptance; how can
you offer any of these to another if you
do not first offer them to yourself?

When what you perceive is over-ridden by
what is...then you are able to see the truth.

What cannot be seen with two good eyes
is often seen clearly by the heart.

The undeniable proof of Universal Love surrounds
you; the way a parent looks at their child, the
way lovers touch, the way old friends greet
each other with a hug. Still need more? Look at
yourself! The Universe created *you* with love.
You ARE its gift of love to your Earth-plane.

Just for a moment...........step outside of yourself and view everything the way The Universe does. View the wondrous dance of your Earth-plane existence. If you allow yourself to see the infinite picture, the dualities and synchronicities, you can choose which to keep and which to change. You are co-Creator!

Your Earth-plane existence is not about where you live, who/what you live with or without, how much you have or do not have. It is about finding what you truly *are*. When you release the responsibility and obligation to BE anything, you move closer to *BE*ing.

What you perceive as the ending of a dream
is, in fact, the beginning of a new one.

Let your thoughts be as fish swimming in the sea, free and flowing with tides. Let your words be like sugar, sweetly pouring forth for all to hear. Let your smiles be tulips, brightening the lives of everyone that gazes upon them.

Guilt is created by feelings of inadequacy.
The Universe created you, even with all of
your imperfections, perfectly. Therefore, your
feelings of inadequacy are self and societally
programmed. If you see yourself as The Universe
sees you, perfect, there is no need for guilt.

Do not be afraid to show your soul to the world. For every one person that turns away, there are ten willing to see, love, appreciate and respect you for who you truly are.

The beautiful moments you can experience on your Earth-plane are limited only by the width and breadth of your imagination.

Shifts in your world are inevitable. Some things remain static, others grow and still others fall away. Do not take it personally.......it is the way things are meant to be. You would not be considered human on your Earth-plane without them.

Spiral out away from your center, grow,
learn, love and be at peace.

Everything you want, everything your heart yearns
for is yours for the asking. ASK and it is so!

There will come a time when what is said about you, who says it and how it is said will not matter anymore. This is called knowing the truth and being at peace with yourself.

A simple act of forgiveness, even if you are not responsible for the behavior, can change your world.

Picture, if you will, the most beautiful movement you have ever seen. With it held firmly in imagination, apply it to your thoughts. The free-flowing movement of thought creates form and form becomes reality..............all with graceful intention.

Break away from moving through your Earth-plane existence mechanically. You are a perfect being experiencing a world most never choose to join. Let color, sound, light, shadow, music, love, feelings and breathing incite a riot of joy in your soul!

If you are able to see the good in another human being, however they may present themselves to you, you will be able to readily recognize all of the good parts of yourself.

Why keep all of your happiness, joy, love and excitement for life boxed up and waiting for the right time? NOW is the right time! Not 'some day in the future' or the next 'rainy day'..............*now*!

Open yourself fully to your world, your
Earth-plane existence! Joy awaits!

What joyous occasion other than breathing? What secret wish other than know thyself? What secret dream other than to love? What secret desire other than to live? Your answers all lie within!

When you question whether you are worthy of unconditional love, remind yourself of this; you are perfect and sacred within the eyes of The Universe.

Take time to recognize that the simplest
things are often the most profound.

You are as bright as the sun in the sky, as beautiful as a rhapsody, loved more than the most enraptured lover could. You are a perfect creation.

Fear is a great motivator. It can get you away from 'monsters', carry you to a safe place and keep you hidden. But, what happens when you want to release fear? It is not a matter of replacing it with something like our friend, ego, but of truly believing you do not need it anymore.

The Universe speaks in many different ways;
light, music, moments, movement, touch, taste,
art. The very act of *you* living is The Universe
expressing perfection in human form.

Since the beginning of time, The Universe has been waiting for the appearance of something beautiful, special, unique and perfect on your Earth-plane. It has been waiting for you!

Every moment of indecision, pain, hurt, anger and sadness you feel is giving you a gift. It is up to you to use your free will; choose to have those feelings to continue or release them to The Universe and allow something better to take their place.

Remember.....with the light of The Universe
surrounding you, you are never alone.

The greatest gifts come from the most difficult situations and questions. Difficult situations: they present themselves as a reminder of what you do *not* want to be, act, react or live. Difficult questions: they present themselves as a reminder that ALL thought can change in a moment. But, it takes *your* participation.

Every day, every minute, every second The
Universe will present you with opportunities
to change your way of thinking from negative
to positive. Will you accept the challenge of
creating a whole new world for yourself?

In denying any part of yourself, you are denying
the perfection The Universe created.

Why try to be like anyone else? You are who you are.
There was only *one* of you created. You are unique,
special and have qualities that no other human on
your Earth-plane has ever or will ever possess.

Respect is defined on your Earth-plane as a proper acceptance or courtesy extended to another. This proper acceptance and extension of courtesy should be a given right rather than an earned one. When you treat yourself with respect, you will automatically treat others the same way.

You are what you think.

It does not matter where you came from, who your
parents or friends were or are, where you are
going, who you are with when you arrive or how
long you have lived. In the end, you are all One.

As humans, you sometimes view the flow of The
Universe as an incomprehensible mish-mash of energy.
Know that all things are placed where they are for
a reason; every experience, every emotion, every
situation. And yes, even you have your place in it.

Oh, to love without walls, boundaries or limitations!
You may not understand it now but, when you
are able to accomplish this, The Universe is
yours.....ask and it shall do your bidding!

Life is not stagnant but fluid; it changes, it
evolves, it grows. You can remain in your own
paradigm, continuing to exist in the world you
created for yourself 'before' *or* you can be fluid;
change, evolve and grow. Release your fear of
being fluid and so shall your life become.

The fear of the unknown is not a fear at all. The fear exists in how you feel you will act in and react to it. People constantly change and so will the situations. Why hold onto the fear of an ever-changing reality? Let go.............just be..............and all will be well.

By refusing to step into whatever you may
consider 'something serious', you are sending
a very clear message to yourself and others; I
am not worth being taken seriously. If this is
how you choose to be perceived, wonderful.
But, who wants to be a 'clown' forever?

Instead of feeling 'stuck' and 'trapped', make a change of thought; you are on a plateau taking a rest until the next leap forward in your Earth-plane existence.

You are worthy of your greatest dreams and your most simple pleasures! *You are worthy* of the gift of giving and receiving love, kindness, honor, respect and admiration.

Say *yes* to your hopes and dreams, say *yes* to your new reality, say *yes* to every magic moment of your Earth-plane existence. Right now!

All exists within you, all exists without you. Wrap yourself in the gentle flow of The Universe. You *are* a part of the *grand* plan!

Your conscious mind need not know your Divine Purpose. Your soul knows and is guided by The Universe. Your conscious mind will take action on what your soul shares with you. Whether a whisper or a shout, it is there. *Listen.*

Your destiny and your flow are not determined by outside forces but, by the ones that exist within.

When you are hurt or in doubt, you will often look to something or someone to 'rescue' you. Acts of supplication are born this way. Instead; look into your heart, listen to the voice of The Universe and let it guide you. You will not need to be 'rescued' because you will be saving yourself.

As it changes and grows, let your soul take on the beauty and form of movement. It will gracefully move you closer to your Divine.

If you have to compromise what you believe in, what you want from your life or what you feel is right to please another, then you are settling for a 'half-life'. Embrace all of you and rest in the knowledge that your growth, and not giving in to the status quo, is paramount on in your Earth-plane existence.

You will, on occasion, forget who you really are.
When this happens, remember that it is only
temporary. Returning to your center is inevitable.

For every 'down' moment you experience on
your Earth-plane, there are ten beautiful ones
that you may have missed. It is all a matter
of where you choose to put your focus.

Living in your 'now' does not mean forgetting your past, nor does it mean stopping the planning for your future. Enjoy the fullness of every moment knowing there is always a more beautiful one coming your way.

Even if you do not know the way, The
Universe is there to show you how to step
into the love that surrounds you.

Leaning on someone does not diminish your independence or your feelings of self-love/worth unless you want it to happen. Having someone lean on you does not make you responsible for their well-being in any way. Light beings, in their human forms, need and want to connect with each other on occasion. There is no shame or guilt in it if the give/take comes from a place of unconditional love.

Respond to hate with love. Respond to degradation
with love. Respond to hurtful words and actions
with love. The very act of returning love to
any negative thing transmutes its energy.

Repair yourself so that you may repair the world.

You will be and are guided to the perfect place, at the perfect time and to the perfect people to assist your growth on this Earth-plane. Look closely, these things are right in front of you.

Sometimes, you have to stand by and watch another's truth unfold. Your involvement in it might dilute, distort, influence, change or dis-create it for them. This does not mean you love them any less, have no desire to help or do not want to share in the experience with them. It shows that you, in all your perfection, want the other to attain theirs in their own way.

You can say, "I hope, I hope, I hope" and the things you want may (or may not) come to pass. Instead.....say, "I do, I am, it is"! Change the thought, change the energy and the reality will change.

For every moment of negative you experience, The
Universe whispers a ten-fold of encouragement.
It is up to you to choose which to listen to.

What you feel, how you act and react, and what you say to another in a negative way is a direct reflection of what you need to change within yourself.

What is very obvious to you might not be to another and vice versa. Bring this into your conscious awareness. Step into the other person's paradigm for a while and take a look around. Seeing things from a different perspective will always help you in your growth process.

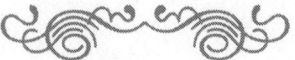

Who, what, where, when and how is not important. What *is* important is to *be;* just be.

Surrendering to the 'flow' of The Universe may feel like a very unnatural thing to do. However, once the release is accomplished, you will find that things will come much more easily than they ever have in the past.

If you choose one thing to be, be stellar! If you choose one thing to say, say a kind word. If you choose one way to act, act honestly and with integrity. If you choose one thing to do, choose to live life the way The Universe meant you to live your Earth-plane existence, *perfectly*!

You are an ever-expanding being of light. Do not try to box, curb, rein in or otherwise stunt yourself. You are made and meant to grow; do it.

You are a piece of the heavens; The
Universe, in human form.

Stretching, reaching, expanding beyond what you felt was possible for yourself, is the first sign that you are becoming what you are truly meant to be.

Be prepared for anything to come to pass; your deepest wishes, your most cherished dreams and your most heartfelt desires. Just think; it is all waiting for you!

Do not believe, for one single solitary moment, that you are not surrounded by the unconditional love of The Universe. It embraces, cradles, nurtures and envelopes your entire being always!

Be authentic in all that you are. The genuineness that you show the world defines you and will determine the path you are to travel.

When you try to control what the conscious mind
perceives as chaos, you will successfully draw more
of it to you. If you surrender yourself to the Love
Power of The Universe, all things become possible.

Printed in Great Britain
by Amazon.co.uk, Ltd.,
Marston Gate.